DELTA BLUES AND HOME SONGS

POEMS

Kraftgriots

Also in the series (POETRY)

Sunday Okpanachi: *A Song for Inikpi*
Ada Ugah: *Colours of the Rainbow*; winner, 1991 Association of Nigerian Authors (ANA) poetry prize.
David Cook et al: *Rising Voices*
Sesan Ajayi: *A Burst of Fireflies*
Akomaye Oko: *Clouds*
Olu Oguibe: *A Gathering Fear*; winner, 1992 All Africa Okigbo prize for Literature & Honourable mention, 1993 Noma Award for Publishing in Africa
Nnimmo Bassey: *Patriots and Cockroaches*
Okinba Launko: *Dream-Seeker on Divining Chain*
Onookome Okome: *Pendants*; winner, 1993 ANA/Cadbury poetry prize
Uba Ofei: *Beyond Fear and Fury*
Abiodun Ehindero: *Response of the Dead*
Uba Ofei: *After the Fire*
Nnimmo Bassey: *Poems on the Run*
Ebereonwu: *Suddenly God was Naked*
Tunde Olusunle: *Fingermarks*
Joe Ushie: *Lambs at the Shrine*
Chinyere Okafor: *From Earth's Bedchamber*
Ezenwa Ohaeto: *The Voice of the Night Masquerade*; joint winner, 1997 ANA/Cadbury poetry prize
George Ehusani: *Fragments of Truth*
Remi Raji: *A Harvest of Laughters*; joint-winner, 1997 ANA/Cadbury poetry prize
Patrick Ebewo: *Self-Portrait & Other Poems*
George Ehusani: *Petals of Truth*
Nnimmo Bassey: *Intercepted*
Joe Ushie: *Eclipse in Rwanda*
Femi Oyebode: *Selected Poems*
Ogaga Ifowodo: *Homeland & Other Poems,* winner, 1993 ANA poetry prize
Godwin Uyi Ojo *Forlorn Dreams*

DELTA BLUES AND HOME SONGS
POEMS

Tanure Ojaide

Kraft Books Limited
University of Ibadan
Post Office Box 22084
Ibadan
Oyo State, Nigeria.

© Tanure Ojaide 1997

FIRST PUBLISHED 1998

ISBN 978-2081-77-9

ALL RIGHTS RESERVED

FIRST PRINTING, NOVEMBER 1998

Computer typeset by MOWA Computers, Ibadan

Printsmarks Ventures, Ososami, Ibadan 02-2318-728

Terror and despotism are always short-sighted.
— Nadezhda Mandelstam

Acknowledgements

I am highly indebted to *Owena* Bruce Onobrakpeya whose art works inspired many poems in the second section of the collection.

Contents   Page

I Delta Blues

My drum beats itself	10
When green was the lingua franca	12
Seasons	15
Wails	17
Immortal grief	20
Delta blues	21
Sleeping in a makeshift grave	24
Elegy for nine warriors	25
Journeying	30
Witchcraft	32
Hallucinations	33
The singer's wish	34
I carry no weapons	36
Fresh casualties	37
I will save my enemy	38
Fetish country	39
The chieftain and his tribe	40
Abuja	41
On solidarity marches	42
Army of microbes	43
Pregnancy of the snake	44
Visiting home	45
Waiting for the next world	46
The prisoner	48
Exceptions	49
A general sickness	50
The desert's not infinite	51
Remembering the town-crier	52

II Home Songs

Climbing the family tree	56
Ayayughe	57

Fragments	59
Dream love	61
Dirge	62
Spaces	66
Dance of defiance	68
Poachers	70
My relatives-in-law	72
My townsman in the army	74
Professor Kuta	76
Odebala	78
Lordship of the leopard	79
Agbogidi	81
Ubiebi fude	83
New moon	84
Aruo-o No admittance	86
Owena's hand	87
Hunter masquerade	89
I, Oniniwherhe, the ant	90
Children of Notoma Street, Warri	91
Serenading the republic	92
Witness the fire: three pieces	94

I
Delta Blues

In memory of Ken Saro-Wiwa and the other eight Delta martyrs.

> If you forget the victim
> of yesterday's sorrow,
> you could become
> a victim of tomorrow.
>
> — Yevgeny Yevtushenko

My drum beats itself

Now that my drum beats itself,
I know that my dead mentor's hand's at work.
This sound I lipsing and others think is mine
could only come from beyond this world—
the little from there makes abundance in my hands.
Inside the drum hides a spirit
that wants me to succeed beyond myself.
I foresee a thunderstorm breaking out in my head—
I wonder how I can contain the gift in lines
that I must chant to earn my griot's name.
I bow to the master who never forgot my service.

If I can wait and listen
Iye iye
Brothers and sisters, if my ears will open wide
Iye iye
If I will sleep awake every season
Iye iye
My people, if I keep my ears primed
Iye iye
I say this because there's another music
 that fills the air but cannot be heard without effort
Iye iye
The deer knows why it only comes out
when the whole world's withdrawn to bed
Iye iye

The air ripples with birdsong,
the tapster's gourd brims over with fresh wine,
and the hunter's god blesses him with a bristling game.
The little from beyond will make abundance in my hands.
My drum beats itself
& I await the carnival the drum divines.
Sing with me

Iye iye, iye iye
Iye iye, iye iye
Iye iye, iye iye.

When green was the lingua franca

My childhood stretched
one unbroken park,
teeming with life.
In the forest green was
the lingua franca
with many dialects.
Everybody's favourite,
water sparkled...
I remember *erhuvwudjayorho*,
such a glamorous fish
but denied growing big.
Earthworm, communal name
for the kind of women seeking
to flourish in soft spots.
Uwara, beauty that defies
tyranny of *Akpobrisi*,
forest manic and recluse—
what flesh or fiber fails
to capitulate before charm?

Snails and *koto* lured me
to tear through tangles
that seasoned my soles
to defy every distance.
Urhurhu grapes coloured
my tongue scarlet,
the *owe* apple fell to me
as cherries and breadfruit
on wind-blessed days.
The cotton tree made me
fly for tossed-out fluffs;
the gum tree took fingerprints
before invisible policemen.
Ikere froglets fell from skies

that covered the land
with tropical sheets;
the skipper-fish overflew
culverts into fisher's ambush.

Undergrowth kept as much
alive as overgrowth, the delta
alliance of big and small,
market of needs, arena
of compensation for all. . .

Then Shell broke the bond
with quakes and a hell
of flares. Stoking a hearth
under God's very behind!
Stop perjuring women for
their industry, none of them
drove God to the sky's height;
it wasn't the pestle's thrust,
that mock love game,
that caused the eternal rift.

Explosions of shells to *under*
mine grease-black *gold*
drove the seasons mental
and to walk on their heads.
Who denies doomed neighbours?
It intensifies with execution
of our very friends; the ogre
closes on every foothold.

I see victims of arson
wherever my restless soles
take me to bear witness.
The Ethiope waterfront
wiped out by prospectors—
so many trees beheaded
and streams mortally poisoned
in the name of jobs and wealth!

And for fear of being counted
in the register of mad ones,
I failed to plant trees
beyond my fenced compound
in the desert-advancing land.
For fear of others' rights,
I left the majority to be
massacred, a treeful carnage.

Now I commune with ghosts
of neighbours and providers
whose healing hands of leaves
and weeds have been amputated.

Seasons

Our towns rose from riverbanks of barter.
Once the waters sustained colouring from oil slick,
our constitution could not remain the same again—
we selected delegates to take our prayers to Abuja,
but guns scared them from the promised land.
If you took fins from a fish, would it still be fish?
If you told farmers of sand dunes that their hoes
couldn't make a dent on famine, they would curse
the oracle for souring their soil with parching winds.

No one doubts anymore the resolve of the season.
The plague from afar has slid in with locusts.
The egrets, orphans since rinderpest days, were
the last of the flock we expected to welcome.
But we faced only one clouded direction
and failed to catch the cries of minority kins.
We clubbed pythons we believed meant evil, but
forgot we were nursing cobras in our closets;
we pay for not heeding our forebears' voices.

No one doubts anymore our irregular habit.
We didn't need to follow the hyena to its house
to confirm the trickster-cannibal we entrusted our fate.
Beware of the smiling face, the slick tongue, and robes!
When you call a thief a thief, he grins and sues
you for libel—he knows the courts are on sale;
police and lawyers wait on litigants in hallways
like vultures overseeing a desolate country.
As she solicits, call the whore by her brand name
and she will summon clients to stone you for harassment.

No one doubts anymore the truth of where we lie.
The flag we fly is a whetstone for matchets, often
bloodied in closed-door rites; it infects with stink.

The priests no longer know the god they worship.
Tell the banjo its strings are too wooden to pluck.
Let slavery's blues not be smothered in the soul!

No one doubts anymore where the Niger flows.
If we had a centaur for president, we wouldn't lose
customs as we have done to the emperor of cackles!
Life would be worse in drought, but it won't be
better in floods; the seniority debate disables.
We spent more than thirty years of marriage
debating whether we should live together or split—
we are fast passing the season of childbearing.
Should scales form the rough edge of our pots?
Should number alone fool us into believing that
giants for all their muscles could not be impotent?
We are a market of acquaintances, bound to
always haggle over what we sell or buy away.

No one doubts anymore the fortune slipping away.

(May 28, 1994)

Wails
*(after **udje** dance songs)*

Another *ANA** meeting will be called
and singers will gather.
I will look all over
and see a space
that can take more than a hundred—
the elephant never hides.
I ask the god of songs
whether all the singers will come,
but that silent space
that can take more than a hundred
stares at me with nostalgia
and gives me a feverish cold.
I won't find one singer
when another *ANA* meeting will be called.

Aridon, give me the voice
to raise this wail
beyond high walls.
In one year I have seen
my forest of friends cut down,
now dust taunts my memory.

If I don't open my mouth,
I will be a dumb-and-deaf
who's unable to forewarn
after a bad dream.
The world needs to hear this:
there's one absent in the assembly,
the singers will never be complete
without the elephant in their midst.

I must raise the loud wail
so that each will reflect his fate.
Take care of your people,

they are your proud assets.
The boa thoughtlessly devours
its own offsprings, Nigeria's
a boa-constrictor in the world map.

Streets echo with wails.
A terrible thing has struck the land,
everyone is covered with shame or sorrow—
this death exceeds other deaths.
They have murdered a favourite son,
this news cannot be a hoax;
for the love of terror,
they have hanged a favourite son
and eight other bearers of truth.
Nobody fools others about these deaths.

The god of songs sobs for a favourite son
and threatens the murderers with repercussions.
None of them will escape the fallout of this travesty
of justice in the name of 'law and order'.
Their heads will be sought everywhere
for the mortal blow they deserve.

Death's such a savage ogre—
show me the road of Death
so that I can take another course.
That's the song of childhood and fear.
Now I will not choose another course
just to avoid death in the right path.

Who will make me laugh,
who will bring *Bassey & Company* to life?
Who will speak to me rotten English,
the lingua franca of the coastline?
Who will tell the forest of flowers?
Who will traverse the darkling plain of the delta?
Who will stand in front as the *iroko* shield
to regain the stolen birthright of millions?
It's for his immeasurable services
that the giant's remembered.
There will be no end to this wail.

"If we had known it would come
to this, . . ." but he's gone—
let no one defile his memory
with regrets and devious wishes.
Death's so impenetrable he hears not.
Nigeria has lost her true diviner
but let no one regret his course.

After the warrior-chief's fall,
somebody else will carry the standard—
Boro left for Saro-Wiwa to take over,
the stump will grow into another *iroko*.
The hardwood shield is broken,
the people are exposed to a storm of abuse;
the diviner's spell is broken
& everybody's left in the open.
But the diviner's words are never halted
by death—*Ominigbo* is my witness.

Capitals carry his pictures
to the clamour of marchers,
the world rebounds with tearful wails—
the death of a king, president, or general
will not raise a tenth of this wail.

There's devilry of soldiers
in this death that exceeds other deaths.
The singers will never be complete
without the elephant in their midst.
Uhaghwa, give me the insuppressable voice
to raise this wail to the world's end.

---

* *ANA* is the Association of Nigerian Authors, which Ken Saro-Wiwa once headed.
* *Uhaghwa* is the Urhobo god of songs and performance, the muse of singers.
* *Iroko* is tropical hardwood common in the Delta area of Nigeria.
* *Ominigbo* in Edo folklore was the diviner who foretold the coming of British invaders to Benin in 1897 and was executed for scaring the Oba. However, as soon as he was executed, the British soldiers appeared and the rest is history.

Immortal grief

"Thank God that people are mortal" (Nadezhda Mandelstam)

One Friday afternoon the sleepful world woke
to the immortal howl of a martyr in the Delta.
The loud Republic now tongue-tied from shame,
the policed cemetery breathless but warm;
there's no door out of the other world to this,
no counsel for wraiths to ease their severed lives.
If there was no death, what other threat
would the uniformed lord wield against mouths
proclaiming the corruption seething from his body?
After presiding over the last primitive act of the century,
he still called out his livery to dance on nine mounds
as if human sacrifice to prolong his rule wasn't enough.
What will he not do, who shat on his mother's grave?
The national anthem's been converted into a dirge,
the women sway to the sad air; the men keep vigil
and grief exhausts the heart with burning rage.
In the frontierless underground, the nine dead snipe
at the lord, shake the executive from sleep—
there can be no sleep after consuming so much flesh
& the insomniac blames his diviners for the sacrifice,
the diviners say they are performing their duty of nodding.
The dead several steps ahead of the lord and his caste
have the advantage of being canonized, unlike those
vultures already rotting before their inevitable end.
Thank God that we are all mortal.

(December 27, 1995)

Delta blues

This share of paradise, the delta of my birth,
reels from an immeasurable wound.
Barrels of alchemical draughts flow
from this hurt to the unquestioning world
that lights up its life in a blind trust.
The inheritance I sat on for centuries
now crushes my body and soul.

The rivers are dark-veined,
a course of perennial draughts.
This home of salt and fish
stilted in mangroves, market of barter,
always welcomes others—
hosts and guests flourished
on palm oil, yams and garri.
This home of plants and birds
least expected a stampede;
there's no refuge east or west,
north or south of this paradise.

Did others not envy my evergreen,
which no reason or season could steal
but only brighten with desire?
Did others not envy the waters
that covered me from sunstroke,
scourge of others the year round?

My nativity gives immortal pain
masked in barrels of oil—
I stew in the womb of fortune.
I live in the deathbed
prepared by a cabal of brokers
breaking the peace of centuries
& tainting not only a thousand rivers,

my lifeblood from the beginning,
but scorching the air and soil.
How many aborigines have been killed
as their sacred soil was debauched
by prospectors, money-mongers?

My birds take flight to the sea,
the animals grope in the burning bush;
head blindly to the hinterland
where the cow's enthroned.
The sky singes my evergreen leaves
and baldness robs me of youthful years.
These are the constitutional rewards
of plenitude, a small fish in the Niger!

Now we are called to banquets
of baron robbers where space's belatedly
created for us to pray over bounties,
the time to say goodbye to our birth
right, now a boon cake for others.

With what eyes will *Olokun*
look at her beneficiaries,
dead or still living in the rack
of uniformed dogs barking
and biting protesters
brandishing green shrubs?
The standard-bearer's betrayed
in the house by thieves, relatives,
& the reapers of the delta crop
could care less for minority rights!

And I am assaulted by visions of
the foreign hangman on a hot Friday noon,
the administrator witnessing failed snaps,
the cries in the garden streets of the port
and the silence in homes that speak loud
in grief that deluged the land's memory.

Those nine mounds woke
into another world, ghostly kings
scornful of their murderers.

Nobody can go further than those mounds
in the fight to right chronic habits
of greed and every wrong of power.
The inheritance I have been blessed with
now crushes my body and soul.

(December 2, 1995)

Sleeping in a makeshift grave

Nigeria sleeps in a makeshift grave.
If she wakes with stars as her eyes,
the next world will be brighter for me and my compatriots.
A gunful of children broke the tetrarch's legs
& the elephant that once pulled the forest along for a path has fallen—
can she get up before she's covered for dead?
If the game's quartered, the delta will be swallowed whole—
the hunters know they only came together for this prize.
You cannot measure the size of the overfilled pits
that trail the boots of strong men that come and go
trampling and thrashing in their ironed uniform.
The hanged men are thrusting their fists from beyond.
The gunners strip their mother before the world,
their undertaker presides over the land with a swaggerstick.
If Nigeria wakes from the grave after the murders,
let the people cast general, staff, and cap
into a marble grave in their born-again memory.
There's no other way to live free here than kill
or be killed. You can tell from our stone country.

(Chicago, December 30, 1995)

Elegy for nine warriors

I

Those I remember in my song
will outlive this ghoulish season,
dawn will outlive the long night.
I hear voices stifled by the hangman,
an old cockroach in the groins of Aso Rock.
Those I remember with these notes
walk back erect from the stake.

The hangman has made his case,
delivered nine heads through the sunpost
and sored his eyes from sleepless nights.
The nine start their life after death
as the street takes over their standard.

The forest of flowers mock
the thief, commander of roaches;
there are some heads like the hangman's
that will never have a vision of right.
What does a crow know of flowers?

When ghosts sit down the executioner,
let him plead for neither mercy nor pity;
the General will meet the Master Sergeant
and share the naked dance to the dark hole.

I hear voices of the dead assault
the head cultist daubed with blood—
he runs from demons of his high command.
The cockroach will not live through the sun
but those I remember in my song—
nine marchers who died carrying
our destiny on their broad chests—
will surely outlive the blood-laden season.

II

The sun's blinded by a hideous spectacle.
And the boat of the dead drifts mistward.
They will embrace the Keeper of *Urhoro* Gate
even as the soil that covered their bodies
despite guards rises into a national shrine.
Birds that fly past click their beaks in deference,
the community of stars make space for the newborn;
they will always light the horizon with hope
& those in the wake who raise grieving songs
will look up to the promise of unfettered dawn,
hope against the rope of the barbarian chief.

III

The butcher of Abuja
dances with skulls,
Ogiso* 's grandchild by incest
digs his macabre steps
in the womb of Aso Rock.
To get to his castle,
you would stumble over skulls,
stumble over jawbones.
With his ordnance of guns,
a trail of mounds; bodies broken
to arrest the inevitable fall.
Flies buzz round him,
throned amidst flukes of courtiers.
Is the prisoner who presides
over cells and cemeteries
not slave of his own slaves?

IV

In these days of mourning
some of my fellow singers laugh.
O Muse, reject their claim on you!

These children who laugh at their naked mother
incur the wrath of their creator-goddess.
They forfeit their kinship, these bastards.

Those whose tribal cackles break loose
as the house's torn with grief
draw on themselves the fate of vultures.

They even ride on the dead
with "Tragedy provokes laughter."
Laughter of the flock of vultures!

They smite the upright ones cut down
in full glare of the noon sun.
Earth and Sky dismayed by the apostasy.

From their corners, they laugh
before somber faces reeling from pain
& mourners can only spit at their noses.

In this suffocating gloom
I turn from my own grief
to weep for fellow singers without a heart.

Only a fool fails to reflect his lot
when an age-mate dies,
& I didn't know there were so many in the trade.

Let no accomplices in the murder
of the Muse's favourite son
think they can fool the divine one.

V

The sorcerer to my shame still lives
as I drown in tears over my brother
he sent away at noon from this world.
The cobra to my shame still lives
as I run from home looking for a big

and long enough stick to smash the demon,
or leave it to suffocate itself with bones.
The world sees the sorcerer's harangues
covering himself with a council of diviners
outnodding their heads in complicity.
He has brought down the eagle
and now plucks feathers off the totem bird!
Does he not know of forbidden acts
that he dismembers the nine eaglets?
He forgets he has left Ken's name behind
& the communal chant of the singerbird's name
rising along the dark waters of the Delta
will stir the karmic bonfire
that will consume his blind dominion.
Surely, that name will be the rod by which
the cobra will meet its slaughter.
The sorcerer to my shame still lives,
but day will surely break over the long night.

VI

We'll surely find a way in the dark
that covers and cuts us from those waiting
to raise the white-and-green flag to the sky.
The eagle nests in the nursery of advancing days.
We'll find a way to reach there
where the chorus rehearses a celebratory chant.
We'll make our way in the dark
but would have lost the fear in our hearts—
the dark will not close eyes
to knowledge of stars, dawn and sun;
nor can it smother the message
of good neighbours, lovers and another country.
No ambush will douse the high spirit
that drives us in the course.
We shall get there
through decades of dark years,
we know we'll have to cross
holes of ambush of hangmen

who do not commit their eyes
to sleep, love and things of beauty.
With the sort of luck we have had
with generals, vultures and presidents,
we'll find a way to reach there in the dark
without government roads and light
but with the rage of being held back
from what we could grasp, stretching ourselves
to the point of exhaustion or death.
None of the survivors will then be
ashamed of being afraid.

* Ogiso: legendary tyrant in Urhobo and Edo folklore.

Journeying

I

Blindfolded, he still jumped over creeks into the Niger.
His vision, that of a crocodile that would not be caught
by the steel net thrown over his lifescape.
He swam underwater in rivers young again,
unclogged and uncovered by a waterfront of sleaze.
A column of helmet-dressed anthills marched through his youth
now a desolate swamp over-ridden by brigades of speculators.
He participated in the regatta of ancestral gods,
his paddles swifter than other rowers can keep up with.
He was the dancer whose abstract mask of innocence
dialogued with the sky lord in a brush of fire.
The tall *iroko* in the forest of flowers,
he chose a raincloud for his crown.
He ran the gauntlet of primitive hunters
& his flesh shines through their cannibal teeth.
Now unemployed fishmongers and farmers
sit in his sand-wrecked boat waiting for the high tide.

II

My wanderings in the bookscape revive my nerves.
Dostoevsky came farther than this, embraced the scaffold
and already felt the rough edges of the long rope
before a dispatch-rider broke in with the counter-decree—
for those seconds, the world froze for an eternity on its feet
and from that I know that one can be born again.
If my reprieve does not arrive from Abuja,
it will come from elsewhere . . .
Eyes glued to the horizon, he wondered
for how long he would wait for the reprieve.
Africans take their time even in matters of death.
I am going to be saved to tell this story of
life after death; their crime, my punishment!

But no one stayed the hangman's hands.
No dispatch-rider waved in a decree
to halt his life from being severed.
And through the mists he passed
to the other world, saved elsewhere.

III

At last the boa-constrictor slides into the river
for the sea-ward journey of another life.
Now the abused cat breaks with domesticity
and flees into the forest for freedom.
All the properties of water join the float
to honour *Olokun*'s groom to the underwater palace.
Even the disappearing birds assemble in sea skies—
all go back to the sea that awaits their remains.

The campaigner dies to launch his grand campaign,
the felon that's now the envy of the sentencing judge;
the prisoner freer than his army of jailers.
The pigmy stands taller than the big ones,
a minority voice sung by the vast world.

They conspired to cut his lashing tongue
but they failed, and his tongue's become
oracular rattles that penetrate frontiers.
Now he achieves the hearing denied all his life,
carrying his desires wholesale on his chest
& inhaling contentment from his pipe.

(January 6–8, 1996)

Witchcraft

No other spell than witchcraft explains
Nigeria's closed eyes in the open world.
Every day spreads such a dizzying cloud
that people trip on stumps of beheaded dreams.
Other elephants pace with strength,
this only rattles the airspace with fart;
there's no cover from the silent infection.
There's an incubus on top of the nation,
wears out the body and smothers smiles.
The bewitched land can no longer boast.
of an erect head on its crooked bushpaths.
Not one day one capital city's
free of the deadening draught
that drips from the top of Aso Rock.
They cannot tell the difference,
moving as they do on their heads;
knocking down as they do their kins
and burying them in laughter.
Shameless flies, they gambol in mud.
.The past of a witch always catches up with her—
Nigeria suffers between life and death.
The rest of the world can only wonder.

Hallucinations

Who will save the quarries
from the legendary hunter
boasting of a charmed life?
With multiplying rations of heads,
the slayer daily chokes the earth.
What incestuous rape in the sun!
Still he laughs and phones his kind,
they toast their longevity
with ever more barbaric contrivance.

Everyone whose mouth's a talking drum
waits for the next turn—
the wind blows, the grass shakes;
the smell of fire whacks the nerves.
How will the hunter know that
he will fail, that every night will expire;
only a matter of now or later?

The hallucinations of the presidency
lead straight to suicide—
think of Master Sergeant Doe,
the long line of mad kings,
& wide streets built on bones
through which sirens now convey
the executive with phalanges of guards.
Black guard dogs have the habit of
holding the mortal bite for their master!

The singer's wish

I beat a calabash and sing for
every ear, but I am not a beggar.
Know that I passed over the court
filled with sunshine and laughter,
passed over my mockers' paradise;
the hot garden that swells the head.
I was not only afraid of court tailors
dressing me as a god that I am not,
or artists retouching my face spotless;
and diviners predicting good tidings
even as the palace crashed over the crown.
I was more afraid of winning every game
against courtiers and losing to my people
and keeping an insomniac's eye on anyone
that envisions paradise on mounds of rivals.
I would rob myself of my voice and songs.
I want to carry the calabash and sing—
no lullaby sends the crab to sleep,
I cannot sleep over the soul's deep wounds;
nor can I throw down the hump, Africa's
crushing bundle, that I carry on my back.
I want to pull every ear to the street
against these multiple afflictions.
Divine ones, see the chieftain dancing
with skulls of my brothers and sisters,
see him serenaded by a company of flies,
that shameless breed of pests.
Without slowing down I passed over
the court filled with worshippers
kneeling on bloodstained grounds,
I came to sing to your hearing
from this lower side of town.
I am still beating the calabash
for which many think I am a beggar

and others that I am mad for the denial.
Divine ones, I have one wish you can
execute: let tomorrow be too long
for who climbed over people
to litter the Niger area with mounds.

I carry no weapons

I carry no weapons or fetish on me,
Uhaghwa clears the way with my songs.
God didn't make me to please everyone,
so many must smart from the sting of my songs.
Let those who will plot against me
open their mouths helplessly
as if burned by ripe pepper fruit.
Their secret will spill into the street
& abort before their unbelieving eyes;
they will never reach their goal
of hurting me and celebrating a coup.
Uhaghwa will open their mouths wide
as soon as they convene in coven.
I will foil their stratagems with
a stream of songs that please my god.
Like thieves who beat a stolen drum,
they will be caught and shunned.
Day or night will give them out
& I will continue to mock them.
Uhaghwa clears the way with my songs
& I carry no weapon or fetish on me.

(December 2, 1995)

Fresh casualties
(after J.P. Clark-Bekederemo)

The casualties are not those
still on their feet though more than half-dead,
they survive in their vegetable state.
The casualties are not those
carrying faces wrinkled from denials,
these will be fine with a sudden lift.
Others now with peeling and dry skins
can be groomed with daily baths and lotions.

But what of the many proud names
that flaunted the flag before the world?
Destroyed by barbarians invited to be allies.
What of the heart that expelled dirt
despite the allure of making love in mud?
Sunk into a *naira*-bed of stench.
What of deference to elders, mothers,
children and the disabled of the land?
Strangled by testy nerves.

The casualties are neither those
who stayed the brunt of fire power,
nor who fled for reinforcement or cover;
but those small things tucked in our souls
that shone through the bodies
and made us upright in a crooked world.
We have become mercenaries
slaughtering the totem of the land
to lavishly outlive a killing season.

I will save my enemy

If I can, I will save my enemy from shame.
It's just not proper to subject them to the un
speakable torture that mocked my manhood.
Day will always break to end the bewitching night.
A butcher gave up his executioner's knife
after a cow tied to a stake looked him in the eye—
whatever he saw there made him think of his life.
Imagine if every safari hunter were hounded
by the herd they decimate for sport!
I will use my life to save my enemy from shame—
I have travelled that shameful territory, stripped
and danced helplessly to laughing drums
to the satisfaction of a local chieftain.
I will not defile my scars and the memory of
marching daily to the gallows for a surprise end—
inflicting shame on a defeated enemy
does not fit the battle-cry for human rights.
I will always try to save my enemy from shame
so that I will not be an accomplice of torturers.
In mufti or uniform, Johnson and Doe were murderers.
This said, only the remnant barbarian of the century
will build a scaffold of dishonour that with his orders
dangle the poet's body at noon for the world to see.
Osonobrughwe, give me a full cup of courage
so that I will not shame my worst enemy in death.

(January 4, 1996)

Fetish country

Inside the rocky cave they offer sacrifices
to the god of power, a cobra with a hooded face.
Piles of bodies deck the altar with overabundance.
The stench from the court shrine asphyxiates the country—
the world fears contagion of gun-festered wounds.
In prayers the people ask for their chief priest
to become the god he serves, lord of dogs.
Soldiers know not how to contradict stupid orders.
The mute carriers turn in their unhappy neighbours
who complain about living in the land of the dead.
Nobody dares in the open to speak ill of the god
whose lightning seeks to strike dissonant tongues.
No patience with cocks crowing for dawn in the night.
If only he could cover the face of the sun with his palm
to fool the world as he does his roundtable of flies!
But the executive hand cannot touch the sky.
The howls of humans awaiting sacrifice are muffled
by drums of acolytes possessed by the invisible face.
There's no end to the demands of crazy gods. . .

(April 7, 1996)

The chieftain and his tribe

A chieftain boasts of herding a far-flung tribe.
His people cannot live without bribes.
He spits at them, still they follow him;
they have given up on where he's going.
Each person has something to trade:
money, sex and power are there to die for;
extortion's the thriving national business.
The men lie on their commodities of women,
who still praise them to revive their courage.
Bearing grudges propels their history—
"Because your Papa shot down my dog,
I will not accept the genius of his grandchild!"
The chief chokes his gods with human offerings;
cavalries of greed crush whoever stands in their way.
The grumbling men are ashamed and turn to their wives;
the abused women give out sex with left and right hands—
none is anymore intimidated by guns pointed at them,
these can be silenced by instantly prepared charms.
The tortoise-brained people invent praise-songs
to get to the leftovers of the chief
who throws confettis of *naira* at them—
he knows no dog will bark with its mouth full.
Do you wonder why the Lord of the Rock
still possesses millions of worshippers
despite the bloodstained soil on which they kneel?
The lord has hired a crop of fortune-tellers,
the gifted children of his victims, to counsel
that more human offerings need to be made
to ensure that he lives and rules forever.
If you accuse the chieftain of being an evil idol,
don't spare his tribe of willing worshippers;
they share the same monstrous faith.

(January 7, 1996)

Abuja

Here where all cardinal points meet in a capital
here where rocks raise homes to the sky
here where the savannah rolls over the soil
the coven where witches plot the demise of others
this is where chiefs celebrate on the sweat of slaves
this is where range chickens consume and scatter leftovers
this is where the hyena's den is guarded by rings of packs
this is where the hyena cornered the hare
and swallowed it, leaving no scent for a trace
this is where the boa-constrictor strangles its catch
this is where robbers boast of their callous acts
& laugh at the plight of a hundred million cowards
this is where the national flag covers a cesspool
this is where a god led his worshippers to die
this is where I weep for my entire land.

(Abuja, May 9, 1996)

On solidarity marches

And hirelings delivered by crosscountry caravans,
prepaid direct from the mint glowing with oil profits,
march without a theme song with state-raised placards
before Ministry of Information cameras and a contented pack
of reporters holding to their *naira*-stuffed envelopes.
But even a fool knows the kind of government
that goes every length to seek congratulations
from a livery that usurps the people's name
for hanging a poet whose offense was crying foul
against a robber baron and his far-flung accomplices.
Agents in embroidered robes, appointees, contractors,
and hands not bothered by eating from a murderer's crumbs
ride through blood for a share of the robber's bounty.
And the recluse, a cockroach in the groins of Aso Rock,
thanks them for standing up to the shunning world.
Bare-bellied marchers are always there for the price
& the commander-in-chief, wealthiest thief-of-state,
spends another sleepless night contriving
another pro-government event, a loyalty march
to Abuja, to bow before legendary dark goggles
as he plunges himself further in the blind course
that holds an abyss for its every rider—
Sergeant Doe's sword rusts from blood below!
As for the flies that follow, let them beware
of being buried alive with their benefactor vulture!
Hunger for power or voracious love of *naira*,
ignominy smears the executive's name
& history will take its revenge, however delayed.

(December 9, 1995)

Army of microbes

To the usurper-chieftain who has set his rabid guard dogs
against streets of impoverished ones

To the uniformed caste of half-literate soldiery
who close people's mouths with trigger-ready hands

To robbers who beat loud the drums they stole
from those they feel are blind and deaf to their loss

To the army of insatiable microbes
that have brought plague to the land

To the ruling council fat in the neck and thigh
but whose plans make wraiths of workers

To those who have creased faces of farmers and fishers
with lines of hunger and pain

To the Hyena and his cavalry of hangmen
that litter the landscape with mounds

To the cabal of loyalty and fealty
that sold the rest for coded Swiss accounts

To the executioner and his legion of praise-singers
who maimed the land's totem pet

To the petty head in his lair of Aso Rock
who spreads sorrow into every home

I say, Shame on you and your kind.

(December 12, 1995)

Pregnancy of the snake

Armed robbers are waiting in ambush
to tear off the womb of the nation for sale.
Police are collecting their only earnings from travellers,
the roads gutted with abundant holes.
Scraps of iron, skulls, and blood cover the soil.
Only forbidden food's available, don't eat
and starve; eat and be sick, a vulture's breed.
A uniformed cabal ride a caperisoned horse to death,
care not whether they are stranded in an eternal cemetery.
A misformed head stands on tottering feet accepting salutes.

Benevolent gods have been silenced and chased off;
in their place an assembly of dumb slaughterers.
Don't mind the panegyrics of vultures by their kind.
They are dead people walking the troubled land.
Already grovelling on the soil, what worse dirt?
The boat cannot sink below the river's bed!

Nigeria already carries a full-term pregnancy
& we wait for more ogres. . .

(Lagos, May 5, 1996)

Visiting home

I have gone back to the spring at its abandoned source
to half-quench my burning tongue—
it's in the ruins of old homesteads that
I seek refuge to sustain the exposed head.
Don't leave Mother for good, she shines,
a glimmering shadow of imperial heights.
I have to dig the land into deep-rooted crops
to erect barriers against claims of famine.
I have to gather intermittent produce
into a perennial harvest of hope.
The euphoria of home warmth runs foul
in the universal face of dire denial—
the elders have fallen into the same pit
as their children, neither can raise the other.
This is not the first season that erased smiles,
only to be followed by the sun of contentment.
But who knows when the love of gods
will overcome the connivance of brute rivals?
My fan has caught fire in the heat,
but I recovered my umbrella before the storm.
In this thirst that ravages my soul,
I stand before the homeland's spring:
I can neither drink of its present state
nor will I throw away the calabash—
I must fashion ways to drink of it
without its dirt, drink it only clean. . .

(Warri, May 14, 1996)

Waiting for the next world

Another world is coming,
let those who missed their way in this
wait for the next chance.

I squandered the resources of youth
in family and communal rites,
I didn't see eyes taunting me
from the schoolhouse of my peers.
If I threw the same stamina as I did
upon the palm oil press upon books,
I would today be a director-general
signing out bounties to my praise-singers!
If as I covered remote farms on jigger-pillaged soles
I went the same length with distant learning,
my chapped palms would today be like ripe bananas.
If only I denied myself the festive table,
I would be leaner and healthier today;
but fated as I was, I ate with left and right
instead of touching only the right.
I cannot now catch up with the demands
of model figures, cruel regimen.
Obedient to custom, I listened to rattles
that summoned me to the communal shrine;
I could not read the clock on the wall
& today I am too late for the assembly of peers.
I cannot play children's games of speed at old age.
I sought the assistance of beatles
& have an empty barn for misjudgement.
I have worked the season inside out
but could not build barriers against fireclouds of famine.
As soon as I set my hooks over dark waters,
the blazing moon zealously rose over them
& I caught no fish where others filled gourds
and made proud names with their record catch.

When I worked hard, I sustained
the disease that disables the strong
& I am still reeling from the blow.

Life's more luck than industry,
more gift than sweat
& between tears and laughter
I came out wet rather than dry.
I don't know what my blind choice
has to do with my life!
I must wait for the next world
to be placed on a soft lot
rather than this rock on which
I can break no grounds.
There must be another chance.

March 3, 1996

The prisoner
(for Gani Fawehinmi)

I

And jail has been his home
more than his self-built house.
They drop him at will in the desert
for sand dunes to bury him alive,
but his soles sanctify the sands
that fortify him to come out of the dead.
They also put him on a rocky plateau
for harmattan nights to freeze his voice,
but he imbibes dew that redoubles his words.
They take him without warrant
and wonder where would still his voice;
but every place now his home,
they keep him in their hands, help
lessly pleading to be rid of his gaze.
And they will only achieve their own end!

II

The ironwood that torments the executive axe,
they thought boulders of Aso Rock would crush him;
but he levelled the sorcerer's dreams with his guts.
They come and come in masked faces to pick him
but he overcomes their craft with his own sacrifice
so huge for most to muster that the rest of us
see a warrior god in a human incarnation—
Ogun holds his shield over orphans of army rule.
I sing of gods as men and men unknown gods.

Exceptions
(for Wole & NADECO activists)

The emperor persecutes the upright clan of diviners
whose words ring ominous bells for his power-play.
If only they would be dogs whose mouths closed with food,
he would stuff them to their necks with the national cake
baked with the same oil that incinerated Ogoni heads!
But they would not taste of forbidden foods that invite the world,
even if it meant they starved and fought with only bones.
They preferred being black ants stinging his buttocks
borne by the high stool that's daily daubed with blood.
The executive of the vast domain of servants and prisoners
looks for ways to break the knees of these irritants.
"Times were when we won wars with all our might.
How can I tear off these fleas from my body without
suffering hemorrhage that will imperil my own life?"
That's grief contained in chambers of the imperial body.
The abused land will remain troubled for a long time.

(April 3, 1996)

A general sickness

One sick man can bury a country with his iron boots,
though he may lack the sense to cover the mass grave.

From the kind of groans the earth has witnessed,
from the faces that have disappeared,
from the blood that has soaked the flag

an evil djinn torments the federation.
Death is a halfblind general lost in politics—
nobody knows all his hands that fan out
to clear the way and dig holes.

He does not like the looks of freedom.
Nor of prosperity and peace & so throws
them into his voluptuous slaughterhouse.

No innocence, no beauty, young or old
moves in his circle of existence—
is it sweat, tears, or acid rain falling
from the brows of subjects?

Birds lose their way in the skies,
on land I return home with a map.
At the intersection of power and greed,
covered by a rock lives the beast.

The head has choked us with poisons
& the land rebounds with insufferable groans.

(Charlotte, June 1, 1996)

The desert's not infinite

From the year soldiers broke out of their barracks
to share the pumpkin and march in a mad frenzy,
the streets felt crushed by their loaded boots.
There's never been a bright day since the first decree—
only soldiers have seen a full moon all the years.
Roads became a string of potholes.
Water hyacinths closed waterways for boats.
Those who caught thieves were jeered at and jailed.
Beetles, rats and mice ruined barns and granaries.
Officers carried potbellies to parade grounds
while an epidemic of anaemia razed ordinary homes.
People were visited by convoys of ailments.
Whoever exercised the right of the tongue cut down,
only cheers of the half-clothed emperor broke the silence.
Nobody knows the government though they say it's there.
The constitution is just the tissue paper of Generals
and the whole country a camp run by their overseers.
Nobody moves outside, except drivers of tanks;
others paralysed and stuck with night for company.
Only soldiers have money and buy love and bread,
all outside their circle look to the sky for signs—
mountain clouds drift from the sea inland
but turn to sand-dunes and bury pilgrim birds;
harmattan winds burn *irokos* and mahoganies.
But every thinking head knows it's a matter of time
for the people to punish soldiers for the murders,
erase the name of the tyrant from the presidency.
Our desert's not infinite, for beyond burning sands
a stretch of green advances from across the horizon.

(Charlotte, June 1, 1996)

Remembering the town-crier

I

When the singer-god's favourite and others
were arrested for murder by voodoo, the world
dismissed it as the joke of illiterate soldiery.
But the head hunter and his tribunal 'followed'
procedure, 'made' a case against the nine
that they 'convicted' and swiftly hanged.
What the lord decrees, there's no appeal!
The men dead, the world woke to the immortal wound.

II

Holed in the South, I am doubly
racked by news from distant home.
Trust the long and evil hands of
military and multinational barons!
Hangings in Nigeria beat the American South
in the non-racial appurtenances of rogues.

III

The sun witnessed the spectacle with clear eyes.
The towncrier dangled from a state-tall post,
a sacred animal caught by a vagabond trap.
We who share the same tenements of the delta
should not lose sight of the tear-logged day.
They could not bear to tear his big heart with shots,
so they chose to bring him down from the air—
human sacrifice to prolong the chieftain's dying rule.
The sun and the world witnessed the spectacle
& we fellow sons and daughters of the trampled delta
must not lose sight of the tear-sogged day.

IV

I know where bones are the only harvest from the soil.
Night summons raise goodbye tears from family eyes—
those driven to desert towns are buried in transit in dunes,
others thrown into bottomless holes beside game reserves.
At day contract assassins escape with their state bonus,
nobody to ask for faces that evaporated from the street.
No mounds to convert to national shrines, though
the subsoil's full to the throat with cadavers.
With wraiths peopling the vast land of my birth
that once grew barns of yams and other staples,
bones are now the only harvest from the soil.

V

A succuba takes over our bridal night—
yet unfathomable faith riding
with pain in one train, not
complaining & forgetting
what we are really waiting for.

VI

Where will bloodless legs
carry one to in this stretch
that runs into the horizon?

VII

The partnership of soldiery and usury
more than racks the land. Sweet Bonny,
a universal delicacy; direct bloodletting.
The superstitious partners throw coins
at the carnage to exorcise wailing spirits,
but no one slain by robbers of guests
would leave murderers to rest with their booty.

VIII

I am Moses but against the law's payback.
I recoil from Doe's end in which Johnson

and his men surpassed the head hunter
in the nerve-wracking ritual of elimination.
Vengeance is sweet, but that's to
the primitive heart we fight so hard against
in the uniformed chief and herd of sharpshooters.
I have witnessed damp cells
and hecatombs of corpses,
but I can only kill in self-defence.

IX

"Who are you to demand payment of debtors
for what they do not owe you but the higher ones?"
I have been charged. I will have to pay a price
to clear the wire-grass covering my inheritance.
Let me join the guild of smiths to forge iron
to break the cycle of "You are wrong and I am right."
I am afraid of stoking hard grudges into an everlasting blaze.

II

Home Songs

In memory of Ezekiel Okpan

When its favourite appears, the cherry tree showers fruits.
— from an Urhobo folksong

Climbing the family tree

I come unavoidably to Grandpa's place.
I knew gin to be his favourite sport,
no party complete without his large frame.
It intrigues me as not the man I knew
when I hear said later that never
lived a man who so desired women.
Perhaps I knew him too late,
only through the morning mist;
after he split rooms with Grandma.
I wonder though what woman would
endure his snores and aftertaste.
But I remember his story of Oruma
who offered a woman a bull but was
passed over for who brought a chicken.
If he had other desires, he must
have covered himself neatly enough
to have intact the one-gate compound
that still binds three generations
long after we gave him the very party
of his life that he would have loved
to celebrate with gin and women
I didn't think he knew all those days.
He always cheered and scared me,
the way he held fire without burning.
As I climb, the sun reflects more
than the tree held for me from its roots.
My love songs are many. I might have
been a drunkard once, but who knows?
And unavoidably, I pause to inhale
and exhale at Grandpa's spot
as I climb the tall family tree.

(May 14–15, 1994)

Ayayughe
(for Anne on Mother's Day, 1994)

You must be Ayayughe
through whose gate every dead
would want to come back a child.
Always waiting for the little ones
never filled from the mother pot,
you bring yam to the table
but never get to eat of it.
You must be Ayayughe
who shames gerry-curled graduates
of the new home school.

I have shamefully heard you felling
a tree for a pestle and a mortar,
I see your hands shuttle daily
to fill five plates with pounded yam.
You always wait for the little ones
never filled from the mother pot,
you half-fainting with smiles
because you are Ayayughe.
You whose multiple industry
runs more than full capacity
must be Ayayughe on every lip.

What wheel from divine pottery
that never fails turning
drives you in this circle where
children play hide-and-seek?
You must be Ayayughe
who break your back lifting
the crisis-ridden produce of our loins.
You who foreknow every shadow, step
and voice in the other rooms and
spring to douse the forehead's fire,
must be no other than Ayayughe.

You must be Ayayughe,
you tethered to the home:
"I can't leave them alone
even for a day's Concord vacation
in London, Paris, or any paradise!"

For all the *male*-information,
I know you are more
the guardian of the home.
And for you, Ayayughe,
let motherhood be daily blessed.

(May 7-8, 1994)

Fragments

I

Now that I presume
I can clear a forest alone,
what hands are mine
to execute the task?

What matchet will I wield
that is not forged outside
but only of my sweat?

Who will not be offended
by the appropriation
of their strength?

How can I sing tales
that berate the tortoise
and yet keep to myself
the food I find in famine?

I cannot presume.

II

Now the rains, who can
stop them?
Ordained by seasons,
they swamp us with frogs.

Who can stop this deluge
of discontent?

Now the night, who can
stop it?
Ordained by daily demands,
night always falls.

Who can stop them
when we built no shelter
with the light
of dry days?

III

And this I have learned:
a wife is never scared
of her husband's nakedness.

I know the great snare
of my people:
throw them poisoned pumpkins
because you foresee
hunger in their palate,
and they would eat and die.
Wriggle buttocks like grubs
before their starved eyes,
and they would fall into a pit.
Offer them bottles of acid
once you divine dry mouths,
and they would choke themselves.

But why should the healer
not know antidotes of poisons,
why should the warrior not know
how to make love with peace?

I am still learning.

Dream love

This night I inspect my house before going to bed.
A lady shows up at the far-end room I thought empty.
Surprised at the strange face, I ask: "Who are you?"
"I am the same one who came the other day."
"Why didn't you let me know of your coming
and that you would be sleeping in my house? Is it
because you feared I would ask you for love?"
"Not at all," she says; "in fact, we are close relatives."
This I don't understand and have no way of knowing.
That's not all. She brings news from the very home
I miss badly. The king without respect is just dead.
Still my clan must start the business of mourning
and both of us know the custom of every burial.
Wake-keeping has been turned into a love feast.
Drink and dance in a frenzy and after midnight
men and women melt from the ground into cars
parked haphazardly under shadows of plantains—
nobody would leave till after the cocks crow.
Once sleeping in my car, I felt rolling down a slope
and in the startled moment of waking, my eyes
caught the shadow of a man and a woman—
splitting from making love, they were fleeing.
I thought nobody should run away from love.
Why make shameful love? I asked myself.
A voice told me that there was something to it.
I look at the girl, she laughs, stares at my eyes
and asks, "Do you take my word or my feeling?
How can I from saltwater be your relative
this far inland, what do you fear in my face?"
She kicks me hard in the groin for being dumb
and I wake without knowing what I should have done.

(May 24, 1994)

Dirge
(for Ezekiel Okpan)

I

No one foresees the *iroko* tree
ever falling even in a hurricane,
no thunder in the harmattan

but they say death leads to life,
hence the living must die.
I think of trees and their stumps.

II

I deployed my faith to the sun
that my song will shine.
Now an orange ball sits on the horizon,
rocked on the blue lap of the sea.
I dialogue with stone and its hard soul,
my head in my hands, deluged.
I hear bells ring in my body
& now no draught slakes my throat
as I cry in flood and drought.

O soul sored by news of this sudden fall,
my palms cover my head from sunstroke
but the pain still rattles the brain.

III

His river evaporated
in one fever
& he fell, the scribe,
short of words
and carrying a cloud
across frontiers of silence.

He will be stone
except for his name.

IV

I sing of ambush
of the company's home guard
as I probed distant worlds.
I was too far away to hear his call
for reinforcements, too deeply immersed
in waters of the midland sea
to hear his last and stifled cry;
too airborne overflying foreign war zones
to fortify my native company.
But even if I were nearby,
how could my hand re-write
the story of the gods' date?

V

I said goodbye
without meaning to separate,
he said goodbye
without meaning to leave.

Now, after he crossed
seven rivers in one stroke
and no more hears daily rattle,
I hear the goodbye
in "When will you visit again?"

What are omens
that do not belatedly
open eyes in hindsight
to a cavalry of fears?
I'll visit again
to see his face,
a mask of dread
that responds
to no one.

VI

What rage can I wield,
I sentenced to life?
What can I inflict
on the supreme mocker
who waves everybody in,
then asks each to leave
without staying their will.
Urhoro, doorway to all,
stay open; but let us
have a full life here.

What right to rage
I driven by the double impulse
to raise my song forever
and to live a chameleon
holding a lamp over
every minute of steps?
The joys of life are small
before the vast abyss ahead;
below, hysteria and helpless cries—
a box of dust for a lifetime's gift!

VII

Another life
of virgin experience
awaits the blind photographer
across the humanscape
of brains and bones,
where he'll regain
sight of astral ones.

VIII

Underground,
he's the photographer
shooting
the akashic record
of a belated destiny.

IX

No lamp saved the pathfinder
from slipping wholesale into the hole,
no call forewarned the traveller
from wandering irrevocably beyond human precincts.
And so he fell to the leveller who shuns predictions.
I left a guard bull at home and felt secure,
only to hear hours later of the capture.
In every defeat, every loss, that threatens
the heart with self-flagellation, there's
no sense in crying, only a bigger heart
to live above scornful trepidations.

X

In the distance dangles the white chalk
of ancestral privileges that I seek
to mark forehead and tongue before
becoming a respondent of prayers.
Yearly I have seen with these eyes
the *egodi* bird reappear—the world sees;
despite its heart beating out of fear,
it crosses yet another threshold
into abundant light and space
before the horizon greys into a rock
to defy its wings, vision, and much-
echoed song of reappearance. . .

Spaces

And the wails still ring loud in the ears
at the indelible vision of the wake—
"This was not my friend, this cannot
be the cheerful face of he who gave out
with both hands as he stood upright."
But the fact leaves no room for denial
and I looked at the ogre that took over,
I looked at the shrunk but stone weight.
No dream for him or me to wake from,
this was no false news to test loyalty;
there was a wake to go through all night.

A generation of friendship doesn't evaporate
with the disappearance of head and feet.
True, his body's no seed planted in the soil
expected to grow into some crop in weeks;
after the wake there's no denial of this blow.
But his space remains, staring naked.
The principal is missing from the trio,
gone beyond the reach of travel.

But that space's never been empty,
memory has kept a live appearance—
see him with his eternal smile, see him
congratulating brigadier and professor;
celebrating the double elevation as his.
He's busier than ever counselling—
I still seek his approval for my judgement.
I cannot hide anything from him—
let memory sit in judgement, I put my case
& accept the wise one's verdict. . .

The unknowing wives wonder why
this gash cannot heal with years.

I remember the jealousies of spouses,
how we talked all night, laughed all day;
not mindful of others who gave us chance
to trade memories, interlocked decades.

Who will know the unfathomable friendship
that a covered hole cannot erase?
Who sees what the two of us carry
through the daily chores of life
because so invisible but crushing?
I have lost the deeper shade of laughter.

(Warri, April 27, 1996)

Dance of defiance

(in response to Bruce Onobrakpeya's artwork)

We sing and dance at wakes,
gaze at the death before us
extravagantly dressed but never appealing—
we pour earth over love when we have to
and leave behind daily scares.
"Tomorrow will spring fresh demands
on those still recovering from this blow."
We withdraw to bed at the end of day.
By break of day there are shoots
out of littering mounds,
flowers that bloom over bones.
The sun has kept the promise!
How will the bride not long for a baby,
though she foresees the stabs of labour
and the risks her newborn will face
to survive the army of child-killers?

I will still climb towards
the thin neck of the magic palm
to get my wine fresh from the top,
though yesterday we buried knife,
gourd, and tapster who fell from the sky.
The soldier goes to war against odds
and fired up, clears what stands
in the way to the victory dance.
Let me be the *eyareya* grass
shaken relentlessly by winds
but will not fall in the frenzy.
Let me be that perennial river
that will be swallowed by the sea
but will continue to swagger
in my course of torrents

heading there, without fear
of infinite waters ahead.

(Reading, PA. September 1, 1996)

Poachers

Iku yegbe!
Yegbe!
Iku yegbe!
Yegbe!

My ears don't play tricks on me,
so I hear right that you are a doctor.
I thought doctors wear white overalls
and heal in hospitals. Now you say
you aren't a doctor of medicine
but of reading for so long that without
glasses you can't recognize your mother.

Iku yegbe!
Yegbe!

I don't understand. Those plane-borne nomads
who speak none of their own languages are
sought after to sing our people's songs from books,
while those who sang from the womb
and in their home tongues, have been shut out;
herded into holes so as not to be heard.

Iku yegbe!
Yegbe!

We sing from our heads, not from books—
my voice rings out of great depths
and cannot be smothered in pictures of words.
Those who are now known rich from songs
need to be taught how to raise the voice,
how to beat the drum to talk and dance;
and keep quiet in *Uhaghwa*'s assembly.

Iku yegbe!
Yegbe!

There are no longer fishermen of honour,
nor hunters carrying a big heart—
they have all turned poachers.
The world's now upside-down—
we must bring it back to its feet, upright.

Iku yegbe!
Yegbe!
Iku yegbe!
Yegbe!

My relatives-in-law

A son-in-law's service for his wife,
they used to say, *is* endless.
That was when parents-in-law
took their sons-in-law as their own sons.
My relatives at Ekakpamre do not
even say "Welcome" to their son-in-law,
as custom demands, when he visits them.
No kola nut, no drinks, nor cash
came from them. Their pockets,
if they have, are stitched tight.
How do you expect a gift
from your son travelled from afar
before welcoming him?
I don't know what they can afford—
they afford nothing but demands
for more and more money.
Who sells counsel to his son?
At Ekakpamre they sell counsel
and the unsellable to their son-in-law.
They are worse than the Nigerian Police
on their too many roadblocks.
They are robbers without arms.
I have never met their kind elsewhere,
these my relatives-in-law, leeches
which when full will drop
and suffocate from greed.
I will keep away from whoever
introduces himself as my wife's relative.
An evening at Ekakpamre
has taught me a scathing lesson.
I have been robbed by my own people.
My service as son-in-law terminates
with this robbery—service like love's
supposed to be reciprocal to be enjoyed.

I cannot be generous to a pack of hyenas.
I must run from my relatives-in-law
as I do from the Nigerian Police
and robbers, they have no hearts.
The hungry have no shame.
It must be desperate need
that drives wretches to rob their son
without even a mask to save face.
Those who don't have money,
when they see it within reach,
lose their senses and do mean things.
I am not surprised.
I pity my relatives-in-law.

(Warri, July 30-31, 1996)

My townsman in the army

I would prefer to remain a captain
than the major-general whose stars
Udi flaunts before the world.
He thinks he deserves his position,
but we know who clears the way
with her body for his rapid advance.
He's risen fast but I do not envy him.
Every year before promotion interviews,
Madam moves from office to hotel,
hotel to office; leaves home for days
and the officer-husband doesn't even
dare ask a question of her absence.
A fool is really credulous. He believes
when she says she's shopping for contracts.
We know what she contracts out!
When the stupid one goes to the mess
for his daily pepper-soup and beer,
he doesn't know others are
chipping away at his right.
The woman enjoys herself, the man
celebrates his accelerated promotion.
Most senior officers above her husband
know the detailed contours of her body,
now *NAOWA* women keep distance from her—
they don't want to be called whores
because of their loose company.
Officers' wives would prefer their husbands
in guardrooms or posted to ECOMOG,
since they don't want them to be infected
with the viruses Madam Udi carries
and gives out right and left to men.
I prefer to remain a captain all my career
than sell my wife for two stars on my uniform.
I pity the husband whose wife is an article

for sale in every *Mammy Market*.
Some people may be very rich but
their wealth stinks and offends me.
The major-general who has not fought any war
sends his wife to battle in bed with others.
I also hear he loans rifles to armed robbers
who bring him returns from their loot—
let him know what happened to Iyamu!
Udi prides himself as a major-general,
but we know the real general in his home.
I pity the cuckold who wears two stars
to cover his stupidity, yet remains exposed.
I prefer to remain a captain of my home
than the general whose bloody stars
Udi flaunts before the laughing world.

(Lagos, August 6, 1996)

Professor Kuta

I would have kept my peace
if Professor Kuta doesn't parade himself
in a field where he doesn't belong.

A trail of hisses always follows the so-called don.
Robber don, adulterer don, don of nothing learned.
If you know Professor Kuta, you would pity him.
He is a robber masked in an academic gown—
if you don't pay five hundred naira for his three-page handout,
he will fail you even if your head is a computer.
Unless you give five thousand naira to change F to A!
Once he asked a female student all over him
after enjoying themselves in the office,
"Na sex I go chop. Bring money jare!"
The student shouted "Rape" but he silenced the committee
set up to probe his indiscretion and *moral turpitude*.

The collar of his shirt is caked with ochre,
the sole of his shoes shines with holes.
Teachers are poor but Professor Kuta's unbelievable.
By the tenth of the month, his eyes are red with desperation;
if you don't give him a gift, his wife won't go to the market.
His car long wrecked, he is pitiable in his long trek.
I will not encourage any of my children to be a professor.
Kuta has lost his mind—he doesn't look better
than a madman or the mechanic in half-clothes.
Those he went to college with drive big cars.
His relatives have confessed to bewitching him,
there's no other explanation for his wretched plight.

He professes poverty, professes robbery of young ones;
professes nothing scholarly—no book to his credit;
of the articles he cites in his cv, three appeared
in *The Nigerian Observer* and *The Daily Times*;

the other two paid for and printed in street tabloids.
Students have discovered his handouts are lifted
from his undergraduate notebooks wholesale.
If one's mouth conferred authority, Kuta would be a professor.
I heard from his colleagues that he has no Ph.D.
but an ABD, he thrice flunked his Ed.D. defence.
Who doesn't know some doctors are impostors?
Tell Professor Kuta to bring his transcripts for all to see.
The sort of Professor Kuta would be better off trading
than robbing students in the mantle of a don.

Kuta is not a professor he calls himself.
I would have shut my mouth to his masking,
if he doesn't parade himself as a university don.

(Lagos, August 6, 1996)

Odebala

Odebala boasts he is rich.
I only hope he knows what wealth provides!
Odebala swaggers, puffs out his shoulders
because he daydreams he's rich.
We know he inherited debts from his father
and his hands are neither strong nor fortunate.
Some people fool themselves, believing
imagining millions would make them millionaires.
They are the mad without rags in our midst.
Odebala boasts he's the town's millionaire,
but watch him. Who knows what he eats
that there's no red but white in his pupils?
He thinks nobody knows, but they say
he can barely cope with his one wife,
falls asleep before she realizes what he's
doing with her; the woman's crying out!
Unless Odebala hides his wealth in coven,
we see nothing of it in this world or in him.
A rich man should provide for an only wife
but Umukor looks like one without a provider—
she wears no slippers, wears no *george*;
her buttocks are melting away from hardship.
When Odebala claims he's rich again,
ask him what rich man lives in a mud house
when even the poor have zinc and block homes?
From today Odebala should shut his mouth
sored with scurvies and a life of hardship.
His 'jumper' slipped from his waist
and behold: a sackcloth for an underwear!

Lordship of the leopard

In moonlight
our hands intertwined
into unbreakable knots
to keep the growling leopard
from breaking into the circle
of the goat's refuge.
There was no Government
with squadrons of police and dogs,
no millionaire general signing
death sentences like cheques
in the playground, but
we foresaw perils of claws.
Though kids then we knew
how to cover our mates
with the ring of our bodies.

We've grown beyond playing
in moonlight,
forgotten the charter
we inherited from birth
to stick together, grains of a rock.
We let off our hands,
dissolved the circle
for the leopard to raid at will.
Who doesn't know in war
a force in disarray's
easy target from every front?
Look at the stragglers of youth
like snakes each on its own
and writhing helplessly
under a brigand's iron club!
No circle kept off the leopard
from mortally wounding Kakanfo
and his harem of Amazon beauties,

no ring forged to keep off the leopard
from devouring the Delta bard
and his flock of songs.

Outgrowing the playground,
no wall blocks the brute;
everywhere wails split ears—
fear spreads fever over day and night.
Surely the brute ranges freely
& the entire world watches
transfixed, diminished...

(Reading, PA. September 2–4, 1996)

Agbogidi

I, Agbogidi, deflected lightning
from the umbrella tree I sat under;
in the clash with thunder I doused it
with a deluge — palmoil ablaze
drew rain, not smoke, from the sky.
When lost in the forest of night,
I witnessed an antelope transform
into a beauty — that's how I married
a sorceress, we owe each other
what we can't repay in a lifetime.
Now my fan's become a matchet
& I clear ailments out of my way.

I was captive of the chief ogre
and in the seven-day trial
lived only on fingers of chalk
instead of delicacies of bondage—
my prayer flew directly to the sky
and I landed at the outskirts of town,
where journeys begin and end.
This world isn't home enough
until the other world savages
and gives you up from its depth.
Where animals talk and you
heed the multitude of mute wits,
you'll have enough counsel
to bypass death's many paths.
I, Agbogidi, always return home.

This light specially held out for me
to see ahead comes with a price
I am glad to pay with a thousand denials—
sacrifice will open its own way through tangles
to the craft of putting the leopard to sleep

in its own den that you convert into a shrine.
I fight with neither matchet nor gun,
carry an invincible shield in the body.
I don't need to wave a firebrand to burn
what my breath consumes with a murmur.
There's an arsenal of words in the tongue.

How can one be invisible
without seeing in the dark,
how can you be the war-god's hand
without being carrier and sacrifice?
I, Ogidigbo, have chosen this course—
I break through perils and arrive home.

(Reading, PA. September 5–6, 1996)

Ubiebi fude

Certainly, the divine craftsman
more than completed the work
with which he wants to be judged!
Ubiebi fude. Ubiebi fowe.
Glowing, luscent and dark,
others pale before you.
You rub lotion of the palm's kernel
that over the years toned your skin
into a shimmering velvet habit—
Earth couldn't be more blessed.
Hair plaited into hornbill locks,
you're *mamiwata* incarnated;
carrying the many gifts of beauty
all over you without effort, calm.
Everything on you so measured
without hands, without rule;
the cartographer's model, you shine
through and command deference.
I have stopped, dazed by brilliance;
I have often missed steps, tripped
over stumps, knocked on people
not to lose sight of you for a minute.
The world sees for itself
the divine craftsman's masterpiece.
Ubiebi fude. Ubiebi fowe.

(Reading, PA. September 7, 1996)

New moon

Emeravwe phru ugo-o!
We welcomed the moon
with jubilation—
children had allies in women
to whom the new moon
must have meant much too.
I didn't know why though
as God's mirror of light
drifted from the far horizon,
married women ran indoors
as we ran wild outside.
We looked forward to nights,
playgrounds lit for activities;
the storyteller would feed us
courses of fantastic tales.
We missed the divine spectacle,
especially in the rainy season
when the moon and the partner
went to bathe underwater
to reappear brighter than ever.
It came back to meet us
after going the regular round
and left us behind, waiting.
Later *alufa** criers in our midst
ushered in the new moon,
promising the beginning
of a feast of rams and rice.
Now the moon still appears,
neon lights burn the clouds
and cover the bride of youth.
Here there's no voice
tearing night with a shrill tongue
to proclaim the arrival
of our constant guest,

ageless, fresh and luscent.
Today at a new moon,
I revive childhood visions,
defy cold winds for
the spectacle of the couple
in a disc home of light
& envision the many children
our allies indoors gave birth to,
after nine moons, a mountain
that wore them out.
The divine guest increased
not only our laughter
but also our fold!
Emeravwe phru ugo-o!

(Reading, PA. October 1, 1996)

Aruo-o   No admittance

Mi kue ibosu vwiyo-o,	I wear neither the red, nor
mi kue ukpebo vwiyo-o.	the white uniform of sectarians.
Ane me rue ogua re Egba-a.	I am forbidden from Egba's shrine.
Mevwe orharha.	I am the stranger.
Agba je dje idimarha	Let them also keep away the larvae
ne evu re ogua re adjene.	from the medicine-man's shrine.
Odie iyeri eje	Not every fish
ariri mue-e.	can be caught with a net.
Ohwunu de she,	When a gun explodes,
odie efoke re arirhiri-i.	fear not for the tortoise.
Ona vaye abo.	This one has eluded them.
Ukpe avwe ame ke vwe da,	Instead of giving me water to drink,
aya jovwo ke idimarha vwo ho.	they left it for larvae to swim.
Obo re se ohwo okpo	What irritates you
ve obo re rhovwo ohwo	and what bites you
die ovuovo-o.	aren't the same.
Ne obara ve ofigbo so.	Think of blood and palmoil.
"Akpo wene"	"Life changes,"
ode omo re omiovwon.	elders impress on all.
Brabo obo ase ke vwe	How many times what I am denied
rhuere rhoma si vwe?	turns out to save me?
Ire sie ero nu	Those we have ignored
cha be ero kue avware.	turn out to laugh at us.
Akpo okokodo,	Life is so deep,
amre oto roye-e.	its bottom cannot be seen.
Me ya sheri	I didn't go far
ogiribo ki hwe vwe-e.	before a thunderstorm soaked me.

(Reading, PA. October 9, 1996)

Owena's hand
(for Bruce Onobrakpeya)

Your hand inscribes on canvas
beauty that baffles the eye,
love and prayers transporting
initiates into skies of desire.

Hands have brought to life
dry grains of dreams,
planted a hard-cleared farm
to sustain the entire body.
Hand-printed, cotton covers
the world with a coat of comfort.

No victories without hands,
no choices without them—
O Urhoro, what story
of my life did I bring
in words or pictures?
I carry a stuffed bag,
weapon against hostilities.

Maker of beauty,
Designer of a world
contoured with birthmarks and beauty spots,
Pathfinder into every land of promise
your right hand is a god
that built his own shrine
with out-of-season colours.

Hands respond
to promptings of powers
and in you, *Owena*,
there are big powers moving you.

As I traverse the world,
my *father* shows the way—
his sacred chalk rubs me;
from his abundance of phials
clears my eyes into an eagle's
and possesses my tongue
into a singing bird . . .

(Reading, PA. September 13–14, 1996)

Hunter masquerade

The hunter washes his eyes with herbs
to see without being seen, a masquerade,
before crossing frontiers for this spectacle
of animals dancing in their forest quadrangle.
Let him watch without carbide light
so that the dancers will not be diverted
from their story-telling experience.
The beauties in worm-glowing night glisten,
the warriors bristle; each dancer triumphant
in legendary steps that defy movement.
Let the hunter though not embrace the deer
because it's so strangely beautiful,
nor purchase the porcupine's phalanges
because he wants to be invincible;
let him know he breathes another world,
lest he become captive of forest spirits—
a tree a rock transfixed by magic.
If you witnessed the joy of others, what
nerves would pull the trigger against
those too happy to remember death?

(Reading, February 5, 1997)

I, Oniniwherhe, the ant

And this, my coveted pain...
In days of record famine,
I am the envy of those too dis
abled by nothing to venture out.
From round-the-clock foraging,
I have brought home a dead locust—
the game like an elephant crushes me.
Watchful wives and children of neighbours
berate their men for sitting and waiting
for taunting death, their doors open.
Times transform the face of manhood,
hence before sunken half-lit eyes,
I, Oniniwherhe, a mere ant
have become the day's hero!
To the starving world, it would be
incurable madness if I threw away
the only grace of my rusty storage.
But other than vultures and flies,
who eats vermin-swarming cadaver?
If I gorged it, I would go faster
than those who hang on thinly
but wish were me half-gone.
Yet in unprecedented days of nothing,
I cannot discard this rotting morsel;
the prize that others think that I,
like a tortoise, secretly live on—
the very pain they cannot read
from across the dead between us.

(Reading, PA. February 12-13, 1997)

Children of Notoma Street, Warri

This street is an open market without wares,
without buyers and sellers; a traffic of dialogue.
Emptied out of one or two-room homes
where their parents compete in breeding,
they cannot be contained in their tin shacks
overheated and unaired from ventless walls
that cannot hold down the armies of brats.
The current pidgin slang makes its debut here.
They play football, kick any leg around, and push.
Others somersault from tyres placed on the road
back to other tyres—they take turns, applaud
success and boo missteps; they always react.
I see the geometric games in which they jump,
hopscotch. All around, restive and restless figures.
They fight and make up, laugh and cry beyond adult ears.
And their parents, without television and radio, cooped inside
prepare the all-day meal that will half-fill their stomachs
hollowed deep from dawn to dusk exertion.
They go in late, after parents are barely done with love,
to end and begin another day with play and
increase alarmingly from the one or two-room homes.
I may not know who of these will make robber,
doctor, lawyer, businessman, or teacher, but
bare-chested children of Notoma Street
have the dogged stamina to succeed with nothing.

(Warri, May 7, 1996)

Serenading the republic

This abused soil,
the republic of my soul,
tingles with warmth
& spontaneous explosion.
The heart throbs,
each reinforces the other
in a possessing rally.
What's beyond reach,
if we build a pyramid
into the clouds?

You would not think
this is a barren country
with this momentous harvest,
you would not think
this is a rotten place
with the glistening display,
you would not think
these are starving people
with thunder in their voices,
you would not think
this is an unhappy land
with this carnival of laughter,
you would not think
these lions came
from loins of cowards,
you would not think
these skyblazing eagles
were hatched on low brushes.

I have witnessed
a giant recoup
after being on life-support,
I have witnessed

a dry river
overflow from a season's storm,
I have witnessed
sky and earth dialogue
in sun and rain,
I have witnessed
pessimists break
the jinx of failure.

I have come here
to celebrate
the warriors' return—
drums beat,
we brandish green shrubs
and dance in the rain.
I am one of millions
keeping the night
awake with songs,
I have seen every face
brighten in the dark.

The touch of this soil
multiplies my energy
into a cosmic piston
& I am young again,
happy to reclaim
my height, my praise-
name in the crowd.

(Warri/Lagos, July 30 – August 5, 1996)

Witness the fire: three pieces

I

The living have stolen the honour of the dead,
their headpieces, busts or full figures
marking streets desolate from live weapons.
There's a dual carriageway to the beach,
execution ground by decree of poachers.
Why on earth will one short-living man
build a hundred-room mansion for himself,
if he doesn't want slaves, djinns and ghosts
to occupy some? The dead must be laughing.

II

I hear the hunter's gun fire—
I am not afraid for the tortoise.
When droves of sunbirds visit the stream,
its water level won't fall even if they have their fill.
Thunder, that stranger to the harmattan,
for all its rumble cannot wake the dead.
Let the tsetse-fly stalk the tortoise,
it will abandon its ambush: hungry.
Nobody yet to boil stone into yam.
I am Akalamudo, tropical evergreen;
I pale before none. Look at me:
I am not afraid of your face or fire.

III

The street is a burnt offering.
Times have changed without love.
Small ones smaller than ever in the fray
but have not been swallowed in the clouds,
only they cannot go far on roads built
to bring them out to work and back home.
There's a shortcut to the cemetery.

now advanced into distant farmlands;
hunters dead beside their dogs and guns—
the warlord rattles the airspace with decrees.
A few antelopes stand on elephants and leopards
but the majority lie crippled by intolerance.
A child's born but has not been named
by parents not sure of seeing the next sun.
The wind still blows, the sky overcast. . .

(Reading, PA. October 11, 1996)

www.ingramcontent.com/pod-product-compliance
Lightning Source LLC
Chambersburg PA
CBHW070946230426
43666CB00011B/2586